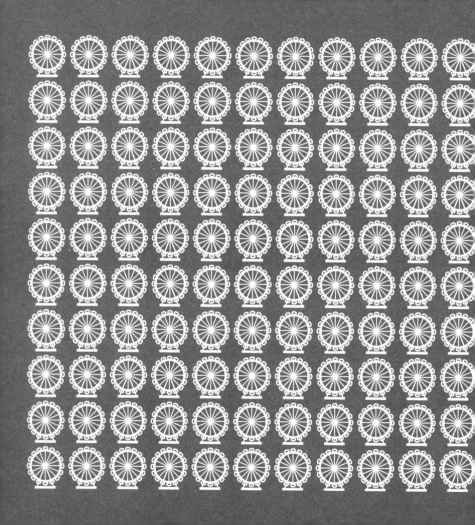

LONDON

LET'S GET QUIZZICAL

GWION PRYDDERCH

SUMMERSDALE PUBLISHERS LTD
46 WEST STREET
CHICHESTER
WEST SUSSEX
PO19 1RP
UK

WWW.SUMMERSDALE.COM
PRINTED AND BOUND IN CHINA
ISBN: 978-1-84953-571-7

SUBSTANTIAL DISCOUNTS ON BULK QUANTITIES OF SUMMERSDALE BOOKS
ARE AVAILABLE TO CORPORATIONS, PROFESSIONAL ASSOCIATIONS AND OTHER
ORGANISATIONS. FOR DETAILS CONTACT NICKY DOUGLAS BY TELEPHONE:
+44 (0) 1243 756902, FAX: +44 (0) 1243 786300 OR EMAIL: NICKY@SUMMERSDALE.COM

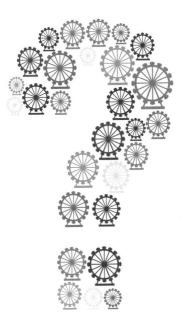

THIS PAIR ONLY APPEARS ONCE ON THE OPPOSITE PAGE

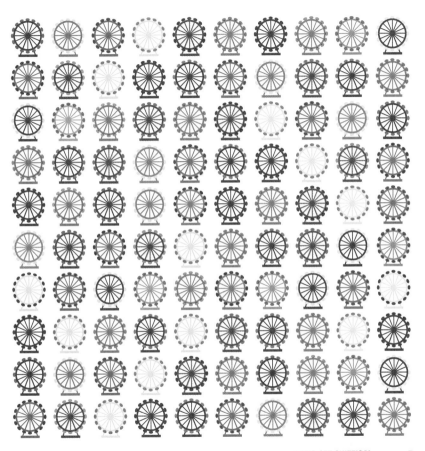

IN AUGUST 1949 WHAT DID A FLOCK OF STARLINGS DO TO BIG BEN'S CLOCK?

A) BUILD THEIR NESTS ON THE HOUR HAND

B) CAUSE IT TO CATCH FIRE

C) MAKE IT LOSE FOUR AND A HALF MINUTES

PICCADILLY
SOHO
SOUTH BANK
STRAND
EAST END
BRIXTON
CAMDEN
MAYFAIR
PALL MALL

```
R  T  Z  L  L  B  E  T  U  P
S  O  U  T  H  B  A  N  K  I
T  H  C  O  T  R  S  C  L  C
R  V  A  K  O  I  T  H  L  C
A  P  M  D  Y  X  E  M  Y  A
N  I  D  A  L  T  N  O  N  D
D  C  E  Y  E  O  D  B  S  I
N  L  N  J  A  N  E  O  O  L
P  A  L  L  M  A  L  L  H  L
M  A  Y  F  A  I  R  G  O  Y
```

WHAT DID A VICTORIAN CLERGYMAN SAY THE CONSTRUCTION OF THE UNDERGROUND WOULD DO?

A) TURN HIM INTO SATAN

B) DISTURB THE DEVIL

C) CONDEMN THE WORKERS TO HELL

SPOT THE DIFFERENCE – THERE'S ONLY ONE!

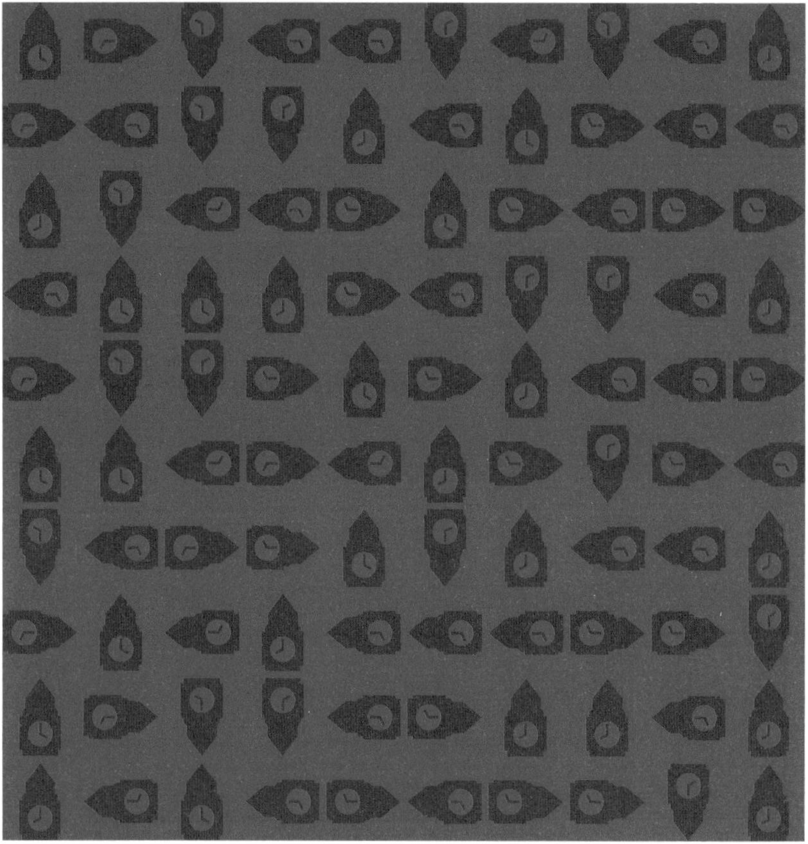

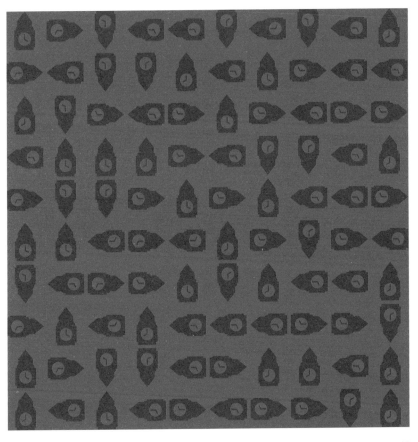

HOW MANY STEPS DOES 30 ST MARY AXE, AFFECTIONATELY KNOWN AS THE GHERKIN, HAVE?

A) 377

B) 1,037

C) 2,450

THIS PAIR ONLY APPEARS ONCE
ON THE OPPOSITE PAGE

THIS PAIR ONLY APPEARS ONCE
ON THE OPPOSITE PAGE

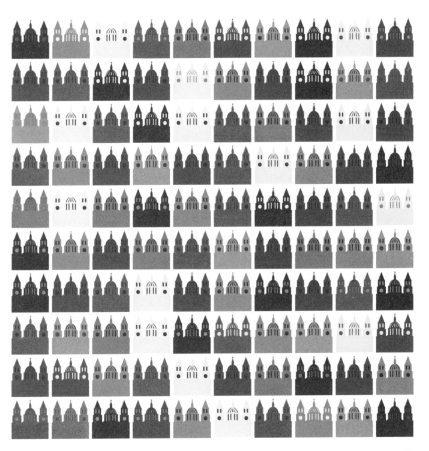

WHY WERE THE TOP-LEVEL OPEN AIR WALKWAYS OF TOWER BRIDGE CLOSED IN 1910?

A) THEY WERE HAUNTED

B) THEY BECAME A HAUNT FOR PROSTITUTES AND PICKPOCKETS

C) TO DEAL WITH A RAT INFESTATION

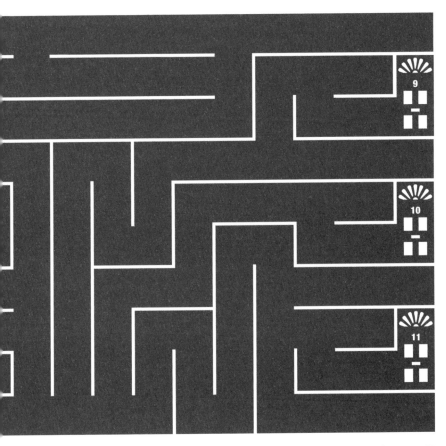

FIND THE 'LONDON' TAXI

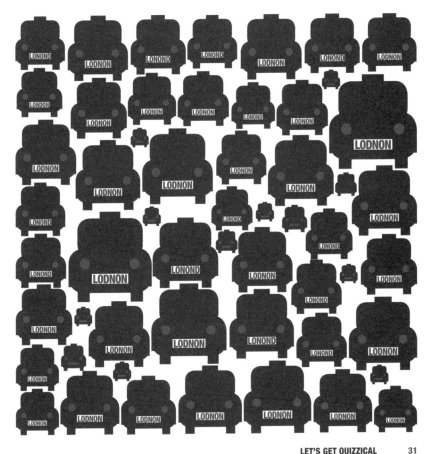

WHAT IS THE NICKNAME OF WATERLOO BRIDGE?

A) THE LADIES' BRIDGE

B) THE KIDS' BRIDGE

C) HARRY'S BRIDGE

SPOT THE DIFFERENCE – THERE'S ONLY ONE!

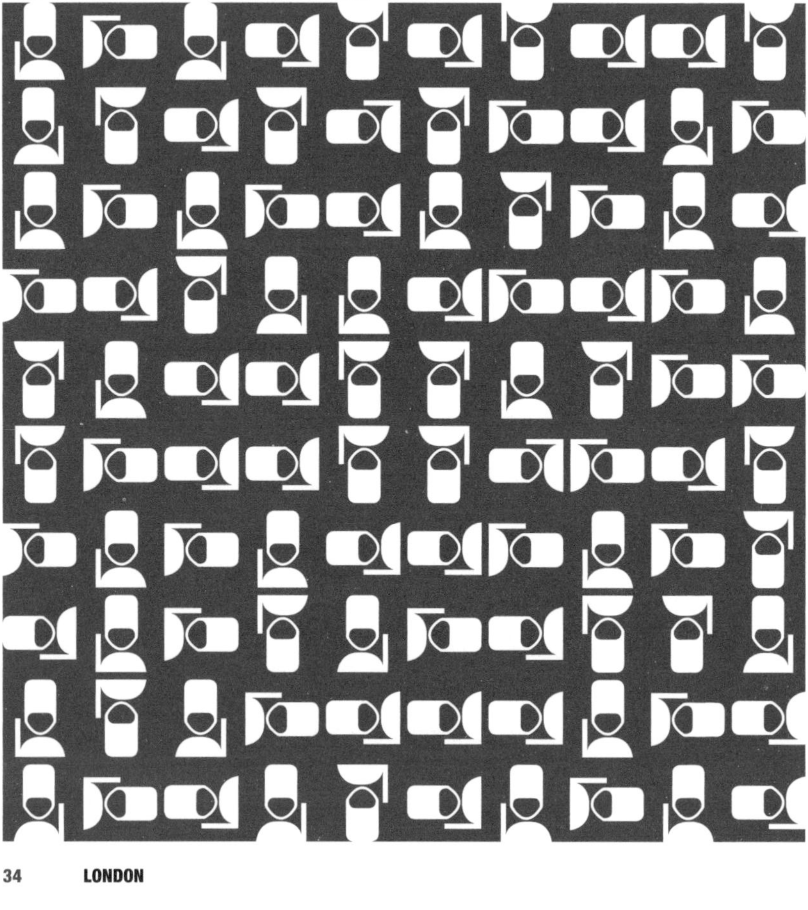

DURING CHRISTMAS 2004 WHAT WAS THE MILLENNIUM DOME USED FOR?

A) A HUGE CAR BOOT SALE

B) AN ICE RINK

C) A SHELTER FOR THE HOMELESS

FIND THE WHITE RAT

WHAT DOES THE HARRODS MOTTO 'OMNIA OMNIBUS UBIQUE' MEAN?

A) EXCLUSIVITY FOR ALL

B) LUXURY FOR THE LUCKY FEW

C) ALL THINGS FOR ALL PEOPLE, EVERYWHERE

SPOT THE DIFFERENCE – THERE'S ONLY ONE!

THIS PAIR ONLY APPEARS ONCE ON THE OPPOSITE PAGE

THE CHANCELLOR
NEEDS TO GET HOME!

GET MY LORD BACK TO COURT SOBER

SPOT THE DIFFERENCE – THERE'S ONLY ONE!

RETURN THE CROWN TO THE TOWER OF LONDON

APOLLO
BARBICAN
DONMAR
GIELGUD
HAYMARKET
PALLADIUM
LYRIC
OLD VIC
PLAYHOUSE
SAVOY

```
M H A Y M A R K E T
P E P E T R A U B I
L Y O L D O N M A R
A O L H O U G E R H
Y S L L Y R I C B S
H N O R L N E I I A
O L D V I C L K C V
U F Q M A X G S A O
S L U U P R U N N Y
E P A L L A D I U M
```

**WHICH FAMOUS LONDON SHOP HIRED
A COBRA TO GUARD A £62,000 PAIR
OF SANDALS?**

A) HARRODS

B) FORTNUM & MASON

C) LIBERTY

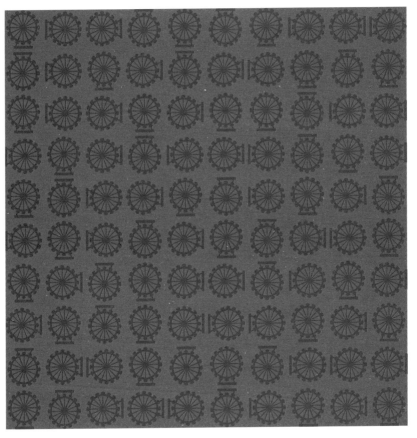

THIS PAIR ONLY APPEARS ONCE ON THE OPPOSITE PAGE

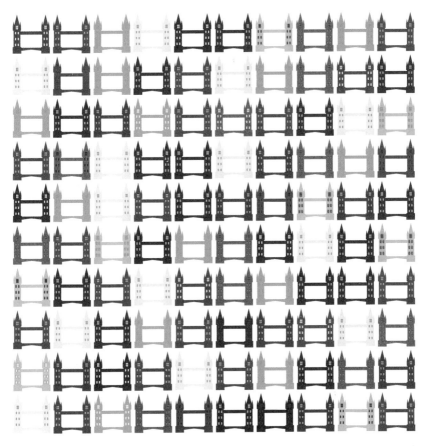

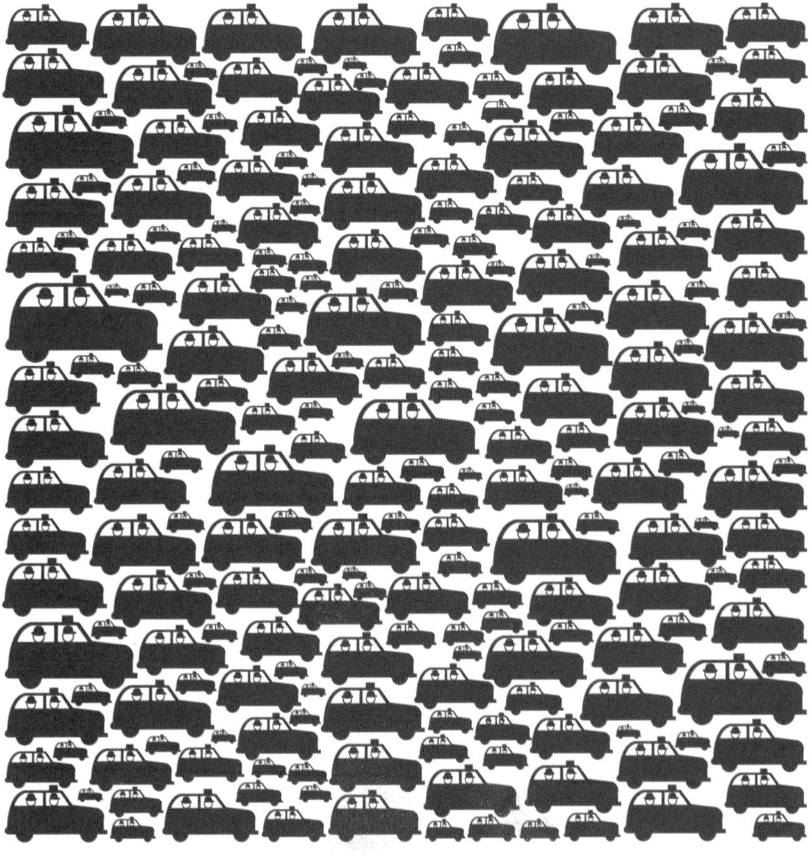

QUICK!
HIS SHIFT STARTS IN TWO MINUTES!

WHICH LONDON STREET IS THE ONLY ONE IN THE UNITED KINGDOM WHERE VEHICLES ARE REQUIRED TO DRIVE ON THE RIGHT?

A) SAVOY COURT

B) OXFORD STREET

C) THE MALL

 **FIND THE PURPLE FISH**

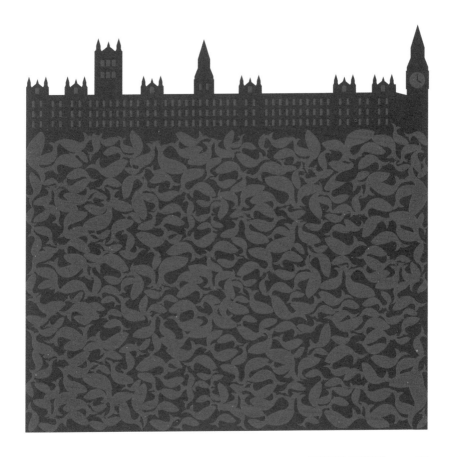

HYDE
REGENT'S
ST JAMES'S
GREEN
GREENWICH
BATTERSEA
VICTORIA
HOLLAND
RICHMOND

```
A  Q  S  Y  J  O  B  N  H  R
V  G  R  E  E  N  A  Y  O  I
I  G  R  O  T  D  T  C  L  C
C  U  E  H  O  U  T  E  L  H
T  B  G  H  Y  D  E  J  A  M
O  C  E  R  L  N  R  I  N  O
R  E  N  S  E  Y  S  K  D  N
I  S  T  J  A  M  E  S  S  D
A  R  S  U  P  R  A  V  Y  E
E  G  R  E  E  N  W  I  C  H
```

FROM WHERE DOES THE NAME SOHO DERIVE?

A) FROM A 17TH-CENTURY HUNTING CRY

B) FROM A ROYAL GREETING

C) FROM A 17TH-CENTURY TOWN CRIER

**THIS PAIR ONLY APPEARS ONCE
ON THE OPPOSITE PAGE**

LONDON BRIDGES

W —————— BRIDGE

H —————— BRIDGE

W —————— BRIDGE

L —————— BRIDGE

V —————— BRIDGE

B _ _ _ _ _ BRIDGE

M _ _ _ _ BRIDGE

S _ _ _ _ _ BRIDGE

L _ _ _ _ _ BRIDGE

T _ _ _ _ BRIDGE

SPOT THE DIFFERENCE – THERE'S ONLY ONE!

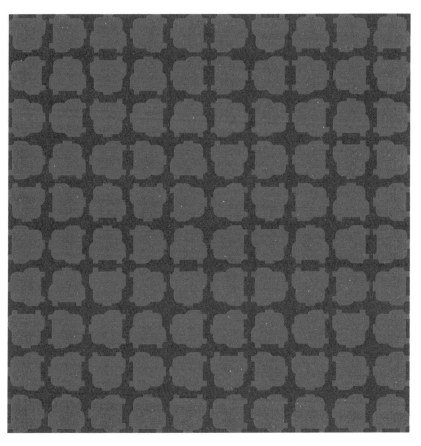

WHERE WAS THE ROYAL COLLECTION OF EXOTIC ANIMALS KEPT BEFORE BECOMING THE BASIS FOR LONDON ZOO?

A) MARBLE ARCH

B) THE TOWER OF LONDON

C) BUCKINGHAM PALACE

THIS PAIR ONLY APPEARS ONCE
ON THE OPPOSITE PAGE

ONE WANTS ONE'S CORGI!

APPROXIMATELY HOW MANY UMBRELLAS ARE LOST ON THE UNDERGROUND EACH YEAR?

A) 40,000

B) 80,000

C) 100,000

 **FIND THE PURPLE PIGEON**

THIS PAIR ONLY APPEARS ONCE
ON THE OPPOSITE PAGE

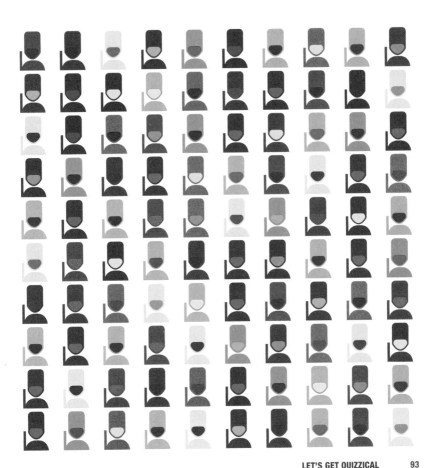

ROYAL ALBERT HALL

WHAT WERE THE THREE SMALL ROOMS INSIDE MARBLE ARCH USED FOR, FROM 1851 UNTIL THE 1960s?

A) A JAIL

B) A POLICE STATION

C) TO STORE THE CROWN JEWELS

IMPERIAL WAR
TRANSPORT
DESIGN
MARITIME
SCIENCE
NATURAL HISTORY
TATE MODERN
BRITISH
V AND A

A	T	R	A	N	S	P	O	R	T
N	B	M	A	R	I	T	I	M	E
S	I	M	P	E	R	I	A	L	S
N	B	H	R	D	D	T	I	W	C
A	R	C	T	O	E	V	O	A	I
T	I	L	I	M	S	K	J	R	E
U	T	O	A	E	I	S	F	C	N
R	I	I	D	T	G	H	C	K	C
A	S	D	V	A	N	D	A	T	E
L	H	I	S	T	O	R	Y	J	R

HOW HIGH IS THE PENTHOUSE APARTMENT AT THE SHARD? (ON A CLEAR DAY IT HAS SEA VIEWS!)

A) 357 FT

B) 537 FT

C) 735 FT

ANSWERS

P4-5

P6-7

![image]

P8-9 C) MAKE IT LOSE FOUR AND A HALF MINUTES

P10-11

R	T	Z	L	L	B	E	T	U	P
S	O	U	T	H	B	A	N	K	I
T	H	C	O	T	R	S	C	L	C
R	V	A	K	O	I	T	H	L	C
A	P	M	D	Y	X	E	M	Y	A
N	I	D	A	L	T	N	O	N	D
D	C	E	Y	E	O	D	B	S	I
N	L	N	J	A	N	E	O	O	L
P	A	L	L	M	A	L	L	H	L
M	A	Y	F	A	I	R	G	O	Y

P12-13 B) DISTURB THE DEVIL

P14-15

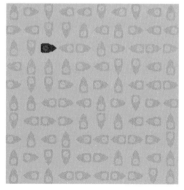

P16-17

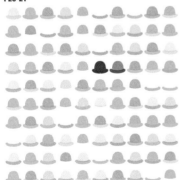

P18-19 B) 1,037

P20-21

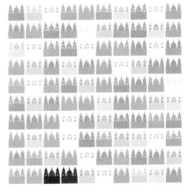

P22-23

P24-25

P28-29

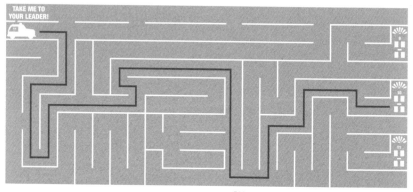

P32-33 A) THE LADIES' BRIDGE

P30-31

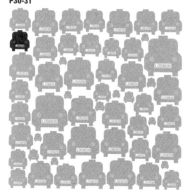

P34-35

P36-37 C) A SHELTER FOR THE HOMELESS

P38-39

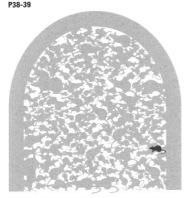

P40-41 C) ALL THINGS FOR ALL PEOPLE, EVERYWHERE

P42-43

P44-45

P46-47

P48-49

P50-51

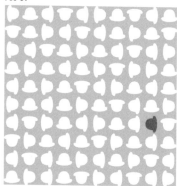

P52-53

P54-55

```
M H A Y M A R K E T
P E P E T R A U B I
L Y O L D O N M A R
A O L H O U G E R H
Y S L L Y R I C B S
H N O R L N E I I A
O L D V I C L K C V
U F Q M A X G S A O
S L U U P R U N N Y
E P A L L A D I U M
```

P56-57 A) HARRODS

P58-59

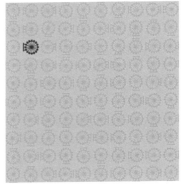

P60-61

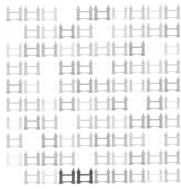

P62-63

P64-65

P66-67 A) SAVOY COURT

P68-69

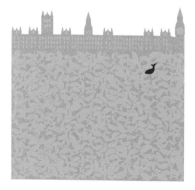

P70-71

```
A Q S Y J O B N H R
V G R E E N A Y O I
I G R O T D T C L C
C U E H O U T E L H
T B G H Y D E J A M
O C E R L N R I N O
R E N S E Y S K D N
I S T J A M E S S D
A R S U P R A V Y E
E G R E E N W I C H
```

P72-73 A) FROM A 17TH CENTURY HUNTING CRY

P74-75

P76-77

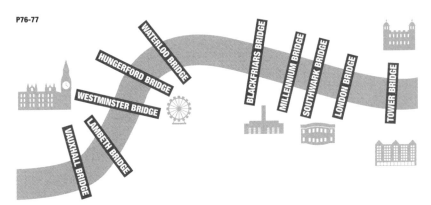

P78-79

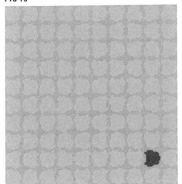

P80-81 B) THE TOWER OF LONDON

P82-83

LET'S GET QUIZZICAL 109

P84-85

P86-87 B) 80,000

P88-89

P90-91

P92-93

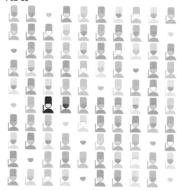

P94-95

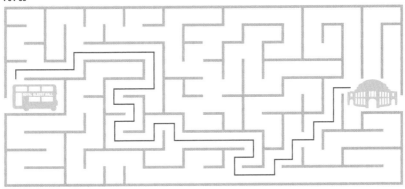

P96-97 B) A POLICE STATION

P98-99

P100-101 C) 735 FT

```
A T R A N S P O R T
N B M A R I T I M E
S I M P E R I A L S
N B H R D D T I W C
A R C T O E V O A I
T I L I M S K J R E
U T O A E I S F C N
R I I D T G H C K C
A S D V A N D A T E
L H I S T O R Y J R
```

IF YOU'RE INTERESTED IN FINDING OUT MORE ABOUT OUR BOOKS, FIND US ON FACEBOOK AT SUMMERSDALE PUBLISHERS AND FOLLOW US ON TWITTER AT @SUMMERSDALE.

WWW.SUMMERSDALE.COM

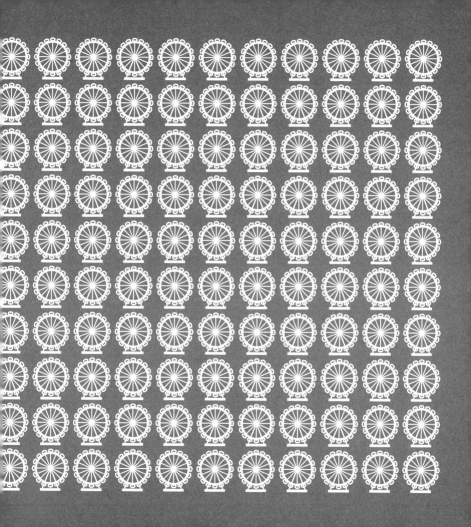

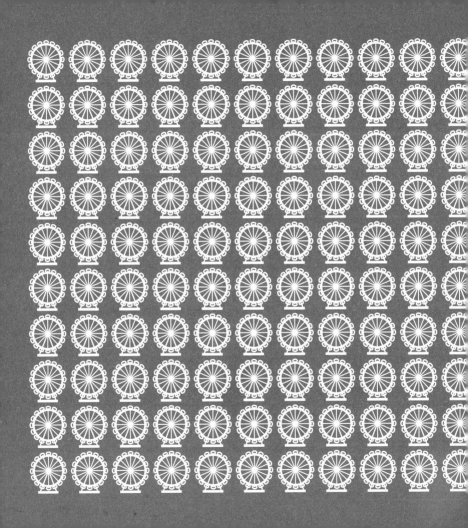